D0570495

$7.00

Palaces of Kyoto

by Tadashi Ishikawa

photographs by Bin Takahashi

 KODANSHA INTERNATIONAL LTD.
TOKYO, NEW YORK & SAN FRANCISCO

Distributors:
UNITED STATES: *Kodansha International/USA, Ltd., through Harper & Row, Publishers, Inc., 10 East 53rd Street, New York, 10022.* SOUTH AMERICA: *Harper & Row, Publishers, Inc., International Department.* CANADA: *Fitzhenry & Whiteside Limited, 150 Lesmill Road, Don Mills, Ontario.* MEXICO AND CENTRAL AMERICA: *HARLA S. A. de C. V., Apartado 30–546, Mexico 4, D. F.* UNITED KINGDOM: *Phaidon Press Limited, Littlegate House, St. Ebbe's Street, Oxford OX1 1SQ.* EUROPE: *Boxerbooks Inc., Limmatstrasse 111, 8031 Zurich.* AUSTRALIA AND NEW ZEALAND: *Book Wise (Australia) Pty. Ltd., 104–8 Sussex Street, Sydney 2000.* THE FAR EAST: *Toppan Company (S) Pte. Ltd., Box 22 Jurong Town Post Office, Jurong, Singapore 22.*

Published by Kodansha International Ltd., 2–12–21 Otowa, Bunkyo-ku, Tokyo 112 and Kodansha International/USA, Ltd., 10 East 53rd Street, New York, New York 10022 and 44 Montgomery Street, San Francisco, California 94104. Copyright © 1968 by Kodansha International Ltd. All rights reserved. Printed in Japan.

LCC 68–17461
ISBN 0–87011–059–4
JBC 0325–780581–2361

First edition, 1968
Sixth printing, 1977

Contents

A NOTE ON THE ENGLISH TEXT

Japanese names are fairly easy to pronounce. Vowels sound much as they do in Italian, while consonants, in the romanization in general use, are not very dissimilar from those of English, save that "g" is always hard. Words tend to be accentless, every syllable occupying much the same length of time, with the exception of long vowels, which double the time, and of "u" and "i," which are sometimes almost silent when they follow "s," "sh," and "k."

In the names given to various buildings of Kyoto's Imperial Palace (in Japanese *Kyoto Gosho*—*Gosho*, or *Goten*, means "Palace"), certain suffixes occur regularly. The most common are:

-den (hall),

-ma (room),

-za (place), and

-mon (gate).

The prefixes *Go-* and *O-* are honorifics.

Palaces of Kyoto

Introduction

When Westerners think of a "royal palace," they usually picture a specific building with a specific name—Buckingham Palace or the Palais du Louvre—but when the Japanese think of their "imperial palace" at Kyoto, they are well aware that it is a whole series of structures comprising a main palace enclosure of over twenty-seven acres, with an outer garden of nearly two hundred and twenty acres. Accustomed to tidy European or American cities, Westerners are never prepared for the vast areas they must cross in order to see the sights of the East. Even so small and crowded a country as Japan imposes this discipline on her visitors.

The first Imperial Palace of Kyoto stood within the Dai-Dairi, the Great Inner Enclosure, at the northern end of the city that was built to accommodate it; later it was moved to the site of a "temporary palace," the Tsuchimikado-den, where it still stands, although, like a living body, it has had to be renewed periodically, and no fragment of the present structure dates from the original palace, however alike parts of it may be in form and material.

Kyoto's Imperial Palace comprises the Shishin-den (or "ceremonial hall"), which was used for all major state functions, and the Seiryō-den ("the pure cool hall"), originally the Imperial living

quarters, as well as some ten other structures. Outside the actual
walls of the Palace stand the remains of the Sentō Palace, in a
magnificent garden, amid harmonious arrangements of rocks,
trees, and water; built originally as a residence for ex-emperors,
it burnt down in the nineteenth century and was never rebuilt,
since there were no ex-emperors to live in it. To the north and
west of the Sentō Palace is the Ōmiya Palace, which Emperor
Go-Mizunoo built in the seventeenth century for his wife, Empress
Tōfukumon-in, and which was later used by his mother, and thereafter every empress-dowager. Today members of the Imperial
Family as well as official guests of the state stay here when visiting
the city.

How lucky we are that Kyoto escaped destruction during the
War! I think perhaps I am not alone among Japanese in believing
that our vast new cities, rebuilt since the War, have been overly
Westernized and have lost much of their Japanese character. But
luckily Japan's two great ancient cities, Kyoto and Nara, escaped
almost untouched, and it is to them that the visitor must go if he
wants to see at first hand a civilization distinctively Japanese.
Kyoto, especially, is rich in so many ways: in painting and sculp-
ture, in Buddhist temples and Shinto shrines, in palaces and castles,
and in gardens—Zen gardens and teahouse gardens. No single
structure, however, expresses more fully the essential nature of
Kyoto (and of Japan) than the Imperial Palace, a quiet, elegant
relic of the past, yet living very much in the present, amid the
shimmering green grass and the pine trees of her gardens, crossed
by paths of snowy white sand and streams of clear water from
Lake Biwa. In the background rise Mount Higashi, with its cele-

brated monuments, and Mount Hiei, whose slopes once housed three thousand Buddhist temples.

It is a unique establishment in that it is the only major palace in the world built entirely of wood—and so, alas, it exercises a peculiar affinity for fire. It has been burnt to the ground many times, and reconstructed each time much as it was before. The Shishin-den, where the present Emperor of Japan was enthroned, is in every essential respect similar to the first Shishin-den erected shortly after Kyoto was founded in the year 794! If its original founder, Emperor Kanmu, were to return to present-day Kyoto for a visit, he would recognize his great hall at once—and perhaps not be so very surprised that it had survived. He might consider, as many modern Japanese do, that that's the way things ought to be. No other country has so strong a veneration for tradition, or possesses the means and the ability to express that veneration, time and again, in the clean, fragile lines of sweet-smelling wood.

Lady Murasaki would feel at home there too, despite the changes that have inevitably occurred since the early years of the eleventh century, when she lived in the Dai-Dairi and depicted its life in her famous *Tale of Genji*. Nor was she the only one to describe Dai-Dairi life: mention may be made of the Kagerō Nikki (the journal of a noblewoman who was known only as "the mother of Michitsuna"), *The Pillow-Book*, Lady Izumi's diary, and *The Tale of Eika*. And there are vivid depictions of daily life, also, in the many painted screens and sliding doors of the Palace that show us hawk-hunting scenes, summer scenes and winter scenes, moon viewing and cherry-blossom viewing. So, one way or another, we know quite a bit about Kyoto during the millennium that it

PALACES OF KYOTO 🍁

flourished and ruled. Nor did it occupy itself solely with government and the arts of war: it is famous for its Buddhist temples and Shinto shrines, its silks and its geishas, its schools and universities—as well as for the fact that it gave birth to the Japanese tea ceremony, to flower-arranging, and to Nō plays.

Although travelers to Japan go first to Tokyo, none leaves without having paid homage to Kyoto. To a certain extent, today, Tokyo *is* Japan, but—in perhaps a far deeper sense—Japan is Kyoto.

1. *Hi-no-omashi,* in the Seiryō-den, often used by the emperor during the day: in the foreground, a brocaded mat on two of the thick mats called tatamis; in the background, "the curtained seat" or Mi-chō-dai, guarded by a lion and a dog.

3. *The Sword and the Jewel,* two of the three sacred treasures that constitute the Imperial Regalia, are housed behind the beautifully painted screens at the back of this matted room in the Tsune-goten, the palace where the emperor actually lived.

2. *Shishin-den,* principal official building of the Palace, contains the throne hall, where the solemn enthronement ceremonies of the emperor are still performed. The courtyard is white sand, and the whole area is bordered by a roofed corridor. To the right is the Nikka-mon, the Sunflower Gate.

4. *Yellow Kerria* around the Old Pond was considered to be one of the ten most beautiful sights of the Sentō Palace grounds. The bridge in the center is made of six large slabs of stone.

History

The reasons that impelled Emperor Kanmu to move his capital to Kyoto are obscure. Some say it was merely because he liked the site; others instance his reluctance to continue under the domination of the Buddhist monks, as he would have had to do if he had stayed at Nara, the previous capital, which had become a city of monasteries; and still others point to the domestic troubles that Kanmu was experiencing at the time. A Buddhist monk had, through the gullibility of the late Empress, made a nearly successful attempt to seize the throne, while the Emperor's younger brother had ordered his trusted steward murdered and had himself died soon after, some said of starvation, some of strangulation. As a result, the Prince's rough and troubled spirit hovered over the old capital, and no amount of expiation seemed to appease it.

The Emperor accordingly, in 784, sent a group of priests to Nagaoka to ask the protection of the local Shinto deity and his permission to settle the court there. This was granted, but the Emperor, nevertheless, decided that he preferred some land about eight or ten miles to the south and west. Two rivers flowed through it, the Katsura and the Kamo, and it was surrounded by mountains

PALACES OF KYOTO ✺

—"a natural sanctuary," as the Emperor himself called it, and an excellent place from which to rule a not wholly pacified country.

A new temple was built on Mount Hiei, to the northeast of the proposed capital, for it was from the northeast that bad luck and disaster came, so a temple to deal with such contingencies was at that time the first step any enlightened ruler would take in planning his capital city. Then priests ensured that the proposed site enjoyed the protection of the spirits of the four cardinal points: the Azure Dragon of the East, the White Tiger of the West, the Red Bird of the South, and the Black Turtle of the North. Finally, east of the site, there was set up a clay statue of a warrior who was to give warning of imminent attack by singing as he moved toward the beleaguered capital.

The Emperor was now ready to begin the building of his palace and of a city to house it. The entire area was to be a kind of rectangle, some five thousand yards from east to west and six thousand from north to south, built on the most enlightened principles of town-planning then available. A spacious avenue bisected the city into east and west sections and led directly to the main palace gate at the north. Six streets ran parallel with this avenue, on both sides of it, while the width of the city was crossed by nine wide avenues. Within the regular rectangles thus formed were numerous lanes for the city's forty thousand houses.

The precise population is, of course, not easily determined, for the earlier Japanese household was far larger than it is today, but historians of Japan estimate that among European cities only Constantinople and Cordova were larger than Kyoto in the ninth and tenth centuries—although Kyoto's appearance could not have been nearly so splendid. The houses were extremely simple—

one-storied and shingle-roofed, and gardens were hidden within inner courts.

The entire city was surrounded by a wall, the *rajō*, which was not like the great stone wall of China but made rather of earthwork and roofed with tiles. However, it had some splendid gates, including that at the south called Rajō-mon (better known, perhaps, as Rashōmon).

At the north of the city stood the Dai-Dairi, a gigantic rectangle measuring well over half a mile on every side. Within it were grouped a large number of government office buildings, palaces of princes, nobles, and dignitaries, official buildings of the Imperial court, and, at the center of the enclosure, the Palace itself, with the Emperor's living quarters, as was customary, at the northeast corner. This was known simply as the Dairi (the Inner Enclosure), and as happens in Japanese, the Emperor generally came to be known by the name of his Palace—he was sometimes spoken of as the Dairi, too. Many of the structures in the compound were joined by a complex system of corridors.

Work began on construction of the city and its inner citadel in March, 793, and by October of the following year was far enough advanced for the Emperor to enter this new capital. Work continued for another thirteen years, partly because of a shortage of funds and partly because of the sophisticated complexities the city planners envisaged for Kyoto. However, by 796, sufficient progress had been made to permit the performance of the New Year's ceremonies in the new city of Heian-kyō, The Capital of Peace, whose name was later changed to Kyoto, from two Chinese characters meaning simply The Capital.

The founder of the city of Kyoto had, suitably enough, before

PALACES OF KYOTO 💥

he had become Emperor, been Principal of the University, and a great student of Chinese civilization. His favorite son, Emperor Saga, was even more deeply enamored of the arts, but also of the graces, of China, and it was he who introduced elaborate Chinese dress and etiquette into the Japanese court. As a result, the cost of living in Kyoto soared; the Emperor's courtiers were unable to meet the expenses of the new way of life; and so began the Imperial custom of granting thousands of acres of tax-free land to favorites —a custom that was, eventually, to put an end to the power of the monarchy and of Kyoto's civilian government.

It was about this time, too, that the famous private schools of Kyoto were founded for the sons of princes and nobles. Instead, however, of devoting their energies to training efficient public servants to administer the government service, the schools were far more interested in the niceties of Chinese court etiquette, in correct clothes and recondite literature. So the country outside Kyoto grew ever more lawless, and the people came to depend, ever more heavily, on the power of the feudal lords, who owned the vast tax-free estates, at the expense of the monarch.

No family was more interesting, in this respect, than the famous house of Fujiwara, which for two centuries controlled Japan, often through marriage into the Imperial family and education of the Imperial children. The office of chancellor was usually filled by a Fujiwara, and if the emperor was a minor, a Fujiwara inevitably became regent. Since their good fortune was so inextricably woven with that of the Imperial family, they supported it wholeheartedly and, although they assumed much of the power it had formerly held, they countenanced no diminution in the respect and veneration it had always received. The Kanin Palace, one of the Emperor's two favorite *sato-dairi*, was originally a Fujiwara property.

The term *sato-dairi* means, quite literally, a "village palace" and was used to refer to any palace in Kyoto, outside the Dai-Dairi compound, in which the monarch took up residence. Originally, he moved to a *sato-dairi* only after fire or earthquake or typhoon drove him out of his own palace. Or if he was forced to go on a journey in an unlucky direction, he slept the night before his departure in a *sato-dairi* facing in a lucky direction. For a time, then, the term was used to mean a temporary residence of the emperor, but some *sato-dairi*, although outside the Imperial compound, served as Imperial residences over such a long period that they lost their temporary status and became, in fact, the Dairi itself. One such was the Tsuchimikado Palace, and another the Kanin Palace.

During the more than four hundred years that elapsed between the foundation of the capital and the beginning of the Kamakura period, the Dairi housed thirty-six sovereigns and was fourteen times destroyed by fire. The first holocaust occurred in the year 960, on the night of October 18, when a strong northeast wind swept the blaze through the entire Palace and destroyed much of great value. The emperor moved to a temporary residence, and ordered his own palace reconstructed. Work began on December 19, 960, and on December 30, 961, he was able to return.

From then on, fires occurred in quick succession, until, by the end of the twelfth century, the Dairi itself, although constantly restored, was in fairly bad shape, and the reigning emperor generally chose to live in some newer *sato-dairi*. Ritual and ceremony tended to follow that which prevailed in the Imperial Palace itself; and essential structures, such as the Shishin-den and the Seiryō-den,

PALACES OF KYOTO 🌿

were built alongside the *sato-dairi*, despite the fact that the real power of the emperor was growing increasingly more circumscribed.

The decline in fortune of the Fujiwara family began with Emperor Go-Sanjō, although his reign, in the third quarter of the eleventh century, was too brief for him to carry out the sweeping administrative reforms that he had envisaged. Fujiwara fortunes declined still further under his two successors, Shirakawa and Go-Toba, who were known as the Cloistered Emperors, for they were nominally monks. They contrived, however, to exercise a certain amount of temporal power and delegated even more into the hands of other Buddhist monks, many of whom lived like the most dissolute of warriors. They kept mercenary troops in the monasteries, and whenever any conflict of interest arose descended on Kyoto with threats of armed intervention. Shirakawa himself remarked that though he was Emperor of Japan, three things in his Empire remained beyond his control: the floods of the River Kamo, the throw of the dice, and the monks on the mountains. But both he and Go-Toba were instrumental in enlarging and beautifying the city's temples and monasteries.

With the fall of the Fujiwara, two other houses rose to prominence, the Minamoto and the Taira, and the power of the court itself declined still further. Inevitably, dissent broke out between the two families, both avid for greater power, both unscrupulous and implacably warlike.

Their precocity in this latter respect is clearly illustrated by one of the Minamotos, a lad of thirteen named Tametomo, who so intimidated his father's household with his combativeness and his physical strength that he was sent off to Kyushu. There, after taking over a band of followers, he married the governor's daughter, assumed the title of Superintendent of Police, and waged open war on many powerful families of the region. The Emperor commanded his father to recall him, but Tametomo declined to be recalled, and when his father was, as a result, deprived of office and power, Tametomo descended on Kyoto with twenty-eight men in time to join his father and brothers in defense of their palace. Then seventeen years old, he was a huge man and used a bow that was eight and a half feet long.

He and his fellow Minamotos, nevertheless, were defeated by the Tairas, who supported the Emperor, and a few years later, after another armed conflict, the Tairas emerged as the dominant power in the country, and the head of the house, Kiyomori, was virtually a dictator until he died in 1181. He was, like most dictators, more unpopular than popular, and on his death left Kyoto in worse condition than he had found it. Not only had fire ravaged it, but Kiyomori had insisted on moving the capital to Fukuwara (near modern Kobe), where he had his house. On his death, the pendulum of power swung again, and the Minamoto, under Yoritomo, regained the ascendency.

This, of course, was one of Kyoto's unhappiest moments, for unlike his predecessors in power, Yoritomo made no attempt to rule from the established capital but decided to set up a military government instead at Kamakura. Although the Emperor and his court remained in their Kyoto palaces, enjoying a frivolous and even luxurious life, the true seat of power was now transferred to the north, not far from the place where Tokyo was one day to be founded, and the country was administered by the army. Thus, Yoritomo removed both himself and his government from the life

PALACES OF KYOTO 〆

of the capital as well as from the temptation to engage in those factional feuds that an idle, well-to-do, and power-hungry society always provides in such great abundance.

The population of Kyoto at this time must have been over half a million. Despite the fact that its power had been so greatly diminished, it was still *the* city of Japan. Kamakura's population, composed mainly of warriors and their followers, was less than half that of Kyoto (although a century later it was said to have greatly increased), while Nara continued to be the ecclesiastical city of Japan.

Although he had been summoned to Kyoto periodically by the Emperor, Yoritomo always contrived to evade the summons. He had, however, out of his own resources, renovated and rebuilt many of the palaces and temples of the capital, and the court's curiosity was aroused by the many rumors that had reached it of the life led by this strangely powerful warlord in Kamakura. At last he agreed on a date to visit the capital, and in August, 1190, architects began the construction of a sumptuous dwelling where he and his retinue might stay.

He left Kamakura on November 2, made a slow tour of inspection as he journeyed, and reached Kyoto on December 5. During his five-week stay, he presented the Emperor with a vast number of extremely costly gifts, and was rewarded with many honors which, according to Japanese custom, he declined. He then returned to Kamakura, and relations between the military camp that ruled the country and the capital that did not continued to be both cordial and wary.

On Yoritomo's death, the power he had exercised passed into his wife's family, the Hōjō, although the court, in the person of an ex-emperor, Go-Toba, made one attempt to wrest it from them. Despite the fact that he had the military strength of the monasteries behind him, the attempt failed, and many of his estates were confiscated. In 1227 the Dairi was once again destroyed, never to be rebuilt on the same spot again. Between 1249 and 1255, Emperor Gofukakusa utilized the Kanin Dairi (which had been rebuilt some forty years earlier) as the basis for his own Imperial Palace.

While Kamakura continued to wield the power, Kyoto continued to live its strangely wasteful, Imperial life, for the highly inefficient custom of putting minors on the throne who abdicated at an early age had now become firmly established. At one time there were five ex-emperors living in the palaces of Kyoto.

Emperor Go-Daigo, however, who came to the throne in 1318, was a grown man who knew his own mind, and shortly after his accession found himself in a bitter quarrel with the Kamakura shogunate over the question of the succession. He was banished to the island of Oki but escaped and with the assistance of certain generals who had deserted Kamakura managed to put an end to Hōjō power and rule. He had the opportunity now to unify the country once again around Kyoto, but he lacked the ability to carry out his obvious mission. After quarreling with the powerful shogun, Ashikaga Takauji, in 1335, he fled from Kyoto, taking with him the Sanshu-no-Jingi, Japan's sacred Imperial Regalia: a mirror, a sword, and a curved jewel.

For the next sixty years Japan was a divided kingdom: Go-Daigo and his successors ruled at Yoshino in the south, where he had taken refuge, while Takauji's puppet-emperor, Kōmyō, reigned with his descendants at Kyoto. The story of the rivalry between the North and South courts is an extremely complex one that ended in 1392, when the South Court yielded and returned the Imperial Regalia to Kyoto.

Meanwhile, the Tsuchimikado-den, a *sato-dairi*, had gradually taken on the role of Imperial Palace. After the Dai-Dairi was abandoned, the Imperial family made use of various Kyoto palaces but at last settled on the Tsuchimikado-den, and it was there that the Imperial Regalia was formally returned to the Northern throne in 1392. This became the Kōkyo, the Imperial Palace, and on that site the Palace remained until 1867.

The man who accomplished the reunion of the two kingdoms was Yoshimitsu, the third Ashikaga shogun, who in the beginning had apparently been an able and efficient reformer and administrator, but whom power corrupted. In the end, his reign was so extravagant that, as one historian put it, the Ashikaga peace was a greater hardship on the people than the long war between the North and South courts had been.

Nevertheless, it was due to Yoshimitsu that Kyoto began to enjoy its renaissance. He built the famous Kinkakuji, The Golden Pavilion, which must have cost well over the equivalent of five million dollars; he restored many temples and shrines; and he encouraged his vassal lords to build ever more splendid mansions. The roofs of Kyoto's palaces, according to a fifteenth-century writer, "seemed to pierce the sky and their balconies to touch the clouds. A lofty hall revealed itself at every fifth step and another at every tenth. . . . " And it was under Yoshimitsu and his successors that Kyoto, although torn by the factionalism and extravagance of the great families, developed Nō drama, gave scope to some of Japan's greatest painters and writers, and perfected the tea ceremony and the art of flower arrangement.

Throughout this period, the Tsuchimikado-den, although accepted as the Imperial Palace, led a checkered, vicissitudinuous life. It burnt to the ground on April 13, 1401, and the Emperor moved out to Yoshimitsu's Muromachi-dai. Using taxes levied on the entire country, Yoshimitsu began the rebuilding of the Tsuchimikado-den on September 10, 1401, and on December 13, 1402, Emperor Go-Komatsu moved in. Some forty years later, on the night of October 16, 1443, an abortive attempt was made to usurp the throne, during the course of which the Palace was once again completely destroyed. This time, the process of rebuilding, due to a shortage of funds, occupied some fourteen years; once again, the Muromachi-dai served as the Imperial residence.

It was in 1467 that Kyoto's long-smoldering factionalism burst into flames, and the great civil war called the Ōnin-no-ran devastated the city. Once again the Emperor took refuge in the Muromachi mansion. As war swept across the city, palaces, temples, and public buildings were razed. After flames destroyed the Muromachi-dai, the Emperor fled to another private house; and after that was destroyed, to still another; and then to yet a fourth. When the war ended, in 1477, Kyoto was in ruins; and the Imperial Palace, although it had not itself been burnt, was uninhabitable.

Reconstruction began on April 18, 1479, and ended February 10, 1480. After an enforced absence of twelve years, Emperor Go-Tsuchimikado was able to return to his Palace, but the work had been skimped: it was not one of the sumptuous Imperial dwellings some of his predecessors had known that this Emperor went home to.

During the next hundred years, the Palace fell into even greater disrepair until it hardly offered shelter against the wind and the rain. Finally the reigning Emperor sent an envoy to Oda Nobunaga, that brilliant and successful warrior, commanding him to rebuild the Palace. Nobunaga entered Kyoto in 1568 and issued instructions for the work to begin; it was completed three years later. Nobunaga, meanwhile, had effected the ruin of his enemies and emerged as the strongest man in Japan; in 1574, he was received by the Emperor in the Palace that he had had restored, where he was offered a cup and the coveted title of Gon-Dainagon. His career ended, ultimately, in defeat and violent death.

But before that happened, Nobunaga had met, encouraged, and assisted the Jesuit missionaries who came to Kyoto to proselytize and who would certainly have been ousted by the Buddhist clergy but for Nobunaga's support. He was never, however, converted, and his friendly attitude toward the Jesuits may have been activated as much by hatred of the Buddhists, who had always been his enemies, as by honest curiosity. In any case, whatever his motives, his encouragement and protection of the foreigners marked a climax in the history of Kyoto and Japan.

After his death in 1582, the capital still lay for the most part in ruins. Although he had rebuilt the Palace and restored some of the temples, the broad avenues were torn up, and the countryside was gradually encroaching on the city. It was not until 1585 that Hideyoshi, a peasant who had been Nobunaga's groom and who took his place as Japan's most powerful man, undertook the total reconstruction of the ruined capital. The city that he built stood for over a hundred years until it too was destroyed by fire in April, 1708.

In 1590, Hideyoshi appointed a commissioner to oversee the

reconstruction of the Palace that Nobunaga had had built and that was now considered to be insufficiently imperial. In October, 1592, Hideyoshi was received by the Emperor in formal audience, signifying that the new Palace was at last ready for occupancy. This was a far larger and grander construction than any Imperial Palace subsequent to the civil war that had broken out well over a century before.

It was not, however, destined to a long life. Tokugawa Ieyasu, after he supplanted Hideyoshi in power, decided for some reason to build an altogether new palace for the Emperor. The year the construction was completed is not known, nor does this construction appear to have been in any way an improvement over its predecessor. It served, however, until 1641, when the Empress Myōsho ordered a new palace for herself.

She entrusted the work to Kobori-Enshū, one of the most famous men of the reign, as well known for his painting and writing as for his skill at flower-arranging and the graces of the tea ceremony. When the Palace was completed, the following year, it was considered to be far more splendid than the one it replaced, and the Empress entered it in state on July 14, 1642. Eleven years later it burnt to the ground.

The new Palace, built in 1654, was destroyed by fire in 1661. Its successor was completed in 1663 and lasted for ten years, when it, too, was destroyed by fire. A new construction was completed in 1675 and lasted until April 28, 1708, when a combination of fire and fierce wind reduced half of Kyoto to ashes. A far larger Palace was now planned; the expenses were to be divided among the lords, according to their revenue; and three lords were commanded to supply fire brigades. This Palace was completed in the same year and survived until the great fire of 1788, one of the most destructive in Kyoto's long inflammatory history.

The capital, meanwhile, had been enjoying ever more ambiguous relations with the West. Hideyoshi, who for a time was master of all Japan, was prepared to tolerate the Portuguese, but he feared the Spaniards; finally he passed restrictive legislation against all Christians and executed twenty-six of them. His successor, Ieyasu Tokugawa, also feared the Church, as exemplified by the Spaniards and the Portuguese, but he was for a time favorably inclined toward the Dutch and the English, to whom he granted various concessions. A proclamation of 1614, however, suppressed Christianity entirely, and Ieyasu's son, who succeeded him in power, was also violently anti-Christian, as were his son's successors.

The Tokugawa court at Edo (later Tokyo) feared foreign aggression and so enacted rigorous anti-foreign legislation. Japanese were forbidden to travel abroad, and foreigners (with the exception of the small Dutch settlement at Deshima) were forbidden to enter Japan—a situation that endured, with few exceptions, until the arrival of Commodore Perry in 1853.

Sixty-five years before this momentous event occurred, Emperor Kōkaku determined, on his accession to the throne, to rebuild his Imperial Palace. The year was 1779; the new Emperor was aged ten. When the Great Fire broke out that destroyed his new Palace, along with two hundred thousand other dwellings in Kyoto, he was nineteen.

The Regent, Matsudaira Sadanobu, came to the capital almost at once, ostensibly to supervise reconstruction of the Palace (but actually, most people believed, to cement relations between the

Imperial Court at Kyoto and the Tokugawa Court at Edo). Shortly after his arrival, he received a secret communication from Emperor Kōkaku (by way of the Tokugawa Shogun, Ienari), signifying the Emperor's desire that the Palace be rebuilt in the antique style rather than in the more recent and customary medieval style. Sadanobu, who was something of an archaeologist, was glad to oblige the young sovereign (and glad, also, to take the opportunity to strengthen the rapport between the two courts), so he called in a Confucian scholar, Uramatsu Kōzen (Kunihiko), and ordered him to take advice from other authorities in the field, so that the new Imperial Palace would be as like the first Imperial Palace as possible.

The site chosen was the familiar one of the *sato-dairi*, the Tsuchi-mikado-den, and despite the unhealthy state of the country, caused by fire and famine, no expense was spared to make the new Palace a place of great beauty, of austere simplicity, of quiet dignity, of impressive solemnity—of the old Japanese way, in other words, a way that had been almost forgotten during Kyoto's more recent and perhaps more sumptuous history.

Work was started immediately: woodworkers and carpenters from Osaka and even faraway Edo were called in; painters, sculptors, and furniture-makers were commissioned; and the Emperor was able to enter his new Palace in September, 1790. He was highly pleased with the result, and even sent the Shogun, Ienari, a Chinese poem in his own hand expressing his pleasure. So it is, in a sense, to Emperor Kōkaku that we owe our debt of gratitude for the antique beauty of the present-day Imperial Palace.

On August 19, 1830, Kyoto suffered a severe earthquake, and the following year a shelter was built within the Palace. It was known as the Jishin-den (which means simply "earthquake hall") and also, because of a nearby spring, the Izumi-den ("cold-water spring hall"), a more appealing name, perhaps, for an earthquake shelter in a place where earthquakes are far too common.

In 1854, the Palace was once again partly destroyed by fire. The Emperor moved out to a temporary palace, and the work of renovation was once again begun. The designs for the previous Palace built for Emperor Kōkaku were closely followed, only a few minor changes being made. A race track was built, as well as a pavilion where the Emperor could watch the races, and, perhaps even more important, a fire station was constructed. On the last day of 1855, the Emperor entered, in state.

Two years before, Commodore Perry made his first appearance at Uraga harbor, bearing a letter from the President of the United States, as well as numerous presents, which he distributed lavishly. He stayed only ten days, but, before he left, announced that he would return the following spring.

Emperor Kōmei, appraised of this catastrophic occurrence, decreed that prayers should be offered at all of Kyoto's chief shrines for the destruction of the barbarian invaders. The Tokugawa court at Edo (Tokyo) contemplated armed resistance but soon decided this would be useless and ordered that the Americans, if they returned, be cordially received.

They did return. In February, 1854, Perry appeared with ten ships and two thousand men and successfully negotiated a treaty of peace and friendship between Japan and the United States. Japan had at last formally admitted the existence of the rest of the world.

Other countries soon followed in America's wake: Holland,

England, and Russia demanded similar privileges. Emperor Kōmei, who was strongly anti-foreign, withdrew from these negotiations, which were concluded at Edo with the shogun. In 1856, Townsend Harris, the first American consul general, arrived at Shimoda, and despite popular anti-foreign agitation succeeded in signing a treaty with the shogun's ministers (and without Imperial approval) opening the port of Yokohama to American vessels. Some time later, Lord Elgin and Baron Gros achieved similar treaties on behalf of England and France, and in 1860 the first Japanese envoys arrived in Washington. They were permitted by the Japanese authorities to stay six weeks.

In Kyoto, the Emperor had ignored all these proceedings. Remaining quietly in his Palace, he became the symbol of popular Japanese distrust of foreigners, while the Tokugawa shogun in Edo rapidly lost much of his following. After the marriage of the Emperor's sister to the young shogun in 1862, he was summoned to Kyoto, where he stayed three months and where he came to an agreement with the Emperor to expel the barbarians. But after several anti-foreign incidents, the British bombarded Kagoshima in 1863, and an allied fleet of British, French, and Dutch ships bombarded Shimonoseki in 1864. The Emperor was forced to withdraw his anti-foreign edict; and after the first British minister to Japan reached Kobe with a fleet of allied warships, the possibility that Kyoto itself might also be bombarded induced the monarch to issue a brief order to the shogun to negotiate such treaties as were necessary.

Despite the Emperor's capitulation, however, Kyoto's lustre remained undimmed, while that of Edo had begun to darken. The era of the shogun was ending at last, and although the Tokugawa continued to fight for their established privileges, they were finally defeated by Emperor Kōmei's successor.

The Emperor died suddenly on February 3, 1867, and his son, Prince Mutsuhito, then fifteen years old, ascended to the throne. He took the posthumous title of Meiji (which means Enlightened Government) and during his reign Japan underwent crucial changes in its political and governmental institutions.

After he abolished the shogunate and moved his capital to Edo in 1869, changing its name to Tokyo (which means "Eastern Capital"), Kyoto's official life came to an end. However, Emperor Meiji decreed that all future enthronements should be held at the Imperial Palace in Kyoto, as they had always been in the past. Consequently, his son, Prince Yoshihito, when he acceded to the Japanese throne in 1912, performed his enthronement ceremonies in the Kyoto Palace, where he adopted, for the title of his reign, Taishō, or Great Righteousness. He died on Christmas Day, 1926, and on November 10, 1928, his son, who had been Prince Hirohito, proceeded to the Imperial Palace in Kyoto for his enthronement.

At ten in the morning, the courtyard of the Shunkō-den was thrown open, to the sound of sacred music as played by court musicians, and the Emperor, followed by the Imperial Family and high officials, entered the Sanctuary. He took his seat in the Inner Chamber, where the Sacred Mirror, a reproduction of the image of Amaterasu-Ōmikami, the first Imperial Ancestress, is enshrined. The Court Chamberlains placed the Sacred Sword and the Sacred Jewel on the table beside His Majesty, as the Empress joined him. The Emperor wore a white ceremonial robe and a black crown;

the Empress wore a white and pink ceremonial robe and carried a white fan.

Then a number of court officials who had been waiting outside the various gates of the Shishin-den proceeded to the east and west verandas of the Ceremonial Hall, and to the inner corridors, and took the places that had been assigned to them, after which the Prime Minister and the Minister of the Imperial Household proceeded to the south veranda. Then the Imperial Princes and Princesses took their places below the front steps of the dais of the Throne.

After the ceremonious entrance of the Emperor and the Empress, the Emperor read the Imperial Rescript, in which he declared, to the spirits of the Imperial ancestors, to the Japanese people, and to the four quarters of the world, the fact of his accession to the throne in 1926. "In building up the Empire," His Imperial Majesty said, "and in reigning over the people, Our Ancestors looked upon the state as their own household and the people as their very children.... This spiritual union between sovereign and people is indeed the essence and flower of our nationality and should remain unchanged as heaven and earth."

The Prime Minister then mounted the south stairs to the veranda of the hall, where he read a congratulatory address, and after descending again, cried "Banzai!" three times, in which he was joined by the entire assemblage. Then the curtains were drawn across the daises, and as the Emperor and Empress withdrew, the Imperial Gongs and Drums were sounded three times, and the Ceremony of the Enthronement ended.

After three days of meditation and fast within the Palace, those entrusted with the Thanksgiving Ceremony began with the performance of purification rites at the Inner Sanctuary of the Shunkō-den on November 13. The following afternoon, at five o'clock, began the Daijō-Sai, the ceremony of offering the first fruits of the harvest to the Sun Goddess, Amaterasu-Ōmikami, and to the deities of heaven and earth; this ceremony lasted until three-thirty the following morning. The saké used was produced out of rice cultivated in a sanctified field and brewed in a Kyoto shrine. A special shrine was constructed for the ceremony—a ceremony that occurs only once in the lifetime of the monarch. The shrine is made of wood, bamboo, and straw; no metal may be used in its construction. These ceremonies were followed by a series of banquets, and the Imperial Palace glittered with moving lights, gay colors, and royal music—as once it had in the past before Emperor Meiji decreed Tokyo to be his new capital.

In 1886, the Palace was officially handed over for safekeeping to the Takumi-ryō, a government bureau established in the year 728, to take charge of festivals and repairs to the Imperial Palace. Part of it is open to the public on weekdays, and a larger area of the Palace is thrown open twice a year, in spring and autumn.

Description

Kyoto's Imperial Palace is enclosed by a tile-roofed, earthwork wall (Plate 5), containing a total area of about twenty-seven acres. The Tsuijibei, as the wall is called, is almost five hundred yards long and some two hundred and fifty yards wide. The shape of the enclosure is rectangular, with a kind of notched indentation at the northeast corner.

The south gate, the Kenrei-mon (Plates 7 and 8), was once used whenever a major state ceremony was to be performed in the main hall of the Palace, the Shishin-den. Now it is used only by the present Emperor, and although it is opened twice a year, in spring and autumn, the public is not allowed to pass through it.

The east wall is broken by the Kenshun-mon, which was formerly used by ministers of state on special occasions but is now the prerogative of the Empress or the Empress-dowager.

Imperial princes and princesses and royal peers used the near west gate, called the Gishū-mon, or Nobles' Gate. It took its name from the fact that the highest ranks of the Court were permitted to ride through the gate in ox-drawn carriages (*gissha*); other ranks, of course, walked. The two additional gates in the west wall, the Seisho-mon and the Junkō-mon, are both of the type called *nikyaku-mon* ("a gate supported by twin columns") and both are tile-roofed. It is through the Seisho-mon that visitors customarily enter the Palace today.

The north gate, the Sakuhei-mon (Plate 85), was reserved for Imperial consorts and their ladies-in-waiting. At the northeast corner of the wall is the unlucky gate, the Kimon (Plate 86), and just beside it stands a carved monkey to keep away demons who might try to enter the Palace through that unlucky gate (Plate 87). In addition to the monumental gates, the Tsuijibei is pierced also by fourteen smaller emergency exists.

The eighteen structures that comprise the Palace are joined by a complex system of covered corridors and separated by characteristic Japanese gardens, with springs and fountains, small streams and bridges to cross them, artificial hills, trees placed with the most meticulous care, and natural rocks to give the gardens their form and shape.

If one were able to enter the Palace through the Kenrei-mon, one would find oneself facing the main gate (the Jōmei-mon) of the main hall (the Shishin-den). The Jōmei-mon (Plates 9 and 19) was opened only on occasion of an enthronement, when members of the Imperial Guard, called Left and Right Soldiers, stood sentinel. Two other gates, invisible from where we stand, pierce the wall surrounding the forecourt of the Shishin-den: the Nikka-mon, or Sunflower Gate, in the East; and the Gekka-mon, or Moonflower Gate, in the West (Plate 20).

Having just entered through the Jōmei-mon, we are now standing in the vast court of the Shishin-den (Plate 2), where certain outdoor ceremonies and special court dances were performed. At the far end, leading to the Shishin-den itself, is a flight of eighteen steps (Plate 18), and as we approach it, we pass two trees —a cherry and a mandarin orange (Plate 10). Similar trees have stood by the steps of the Shishin-den since it was first built and have been replaced as often as they have died.

The word *shishin* represents, apparently, the Chinese expression *tzu-ch'en*, which designated the Imperial court, and *den* in Japanese means a great hall or a palace. Of the various buildings in the Imperial Palace denominated "den," the two most important were the Shishin-den and the Seiryō-den. When the Palace was first built, in the Heian period, an official building known as the Chōdō-in served for the conducting of the most important state business, and its center, the Daigoku-den, was used for coronation ceremonies, but after the abdication of Emperor Takakura (in 1180) the Chōdō-in burnt down and was never rebuilt. From that time on, the Shishin-den became the chief building of the Palace and was considered to be its very heart and soul.

It is about a hundred feet long and just over seventy feet wide. Its enclosing corridors are of red-lacquered wood, with tiled roofs, but the Shishin-den itself is built of unpainted wood, with a board floor and thatched roof of cypress bark. The central hall is called, as in all buildings of this type, the *moya*, and the corridors that surround it on all sides are known as *hisashi*. A small veranda outside the *hisashi* is called the *sunoko*. The windows in these walls are simple, rectangular panels of wooden latticework; they are opened by raising the top half with an ordinary rod.

The name of the north corridor of the Shishin-den is the Gogo, which means "the *hisashi* behind the Emperor's throne," and the eight sliding doors between the Gogo and the main hall have a special name too—the Kenjō-no-Shōji, "sliding doors of the wise men" (Plates 14 and 15), first painted by Kose Kanaoka. No authenticated works of Kanaoka's are extant, and the present-day doors are copies made in the beginning of the nineteenth century. The backs of the doors are decorated with paintings of peacocks and peonies. Between the fourth and fifth doors on either side of the hall is another pair of sliding doors used as entranceways. On the eastern pair are painted the guardian dogs of the Palace; lions figure on the western pair; and above them are the turtles that symbolize happiness and longevity.

On a dais in the center of the Shishin-den stand the Throne and the Curtained Throne (Plates 11, 13, and 16), the former was constructed in antique style especially for the enthronement ceremonies of Emperor Taishō in November, 1915. His father, Emperor Meiji, having decreed that all Imperial coronations take place in the Shishin-den, this was the throne used by both Emperor Taishō and his son, the reigning Emperor, for their enthronement ceremonies. Silk curtains surround the Curtained Throne, and its entrance is guarded by a lion and a dog.

At the end of a roofed corridor (Plate 22), leading from the southeast corner of the Shinshin-den, there lies a plain piece of stone known as the Kiboku-no-Za, "The Place of Divination by Tortoiseshell." After the shell was burnt, the crack that appeared indicated the direction in which a sacred rice field, dedicated to the Imperial Ancestral Shrine, was to be planted. North, across a garden, stands the Jin-no-Za, an unmatted room now reserved for the Imperial bodyguard (Plate 21).

Beyond the Nikka-mon stands the Giyō-den, which was used as a waiting room for ministers of the Crown, when ceremonies were held in the Shishin-den. A minister (Plate 56) would be summoned to the Imperial presence by a lady-in-waiting wearing the colorful *jūnihitoe* (Plate 34) who stood at the east end of the Shishin-den's south porch. The scene is beautifully illustrated in a documentary scroll depicting the coronation of Emperor Kōmei (Plate 12).

An earthwork corridor pierced by two gates links the Shishin-den to the Seiryō-den, which lies to the north and west and has a facade facing east (Plate 24). Like the Shishin-den, the Seiryō-den consists of a central hall, the *moya*, with corridors (*hisashi*) around it, and the whole encircled by eaved verandas, the *sunoko-en*. All the corridors are supported by columns except the east one (Plate 25), which uses pillars and stands exposed to the air. In the center of the east corridor is the Hi-no-Omashi ("a room for the daytime"), and beyond it the Futama, where prayers were said against illness and death. To the north stood an Imperial bedroom called the Yon-no-Otodo (Plate 29).

If one were being received by the emperor in the Seiryō-den, one mounted a stairway below the east corridor, one step of which made a sound as it was walked on which announced the arrival of a visitor.

The central room in the north wing was reserved for the emperor himself, while the rooms on either side were used by Imperial consorts and their ladies (Plate 30).

The southern wing, called the Denjō-no-Ma, served as the Imperial offices, and here ministerial meetings were held (Plate 45). The Kurōdo-dokoro, a bureau created in the year 810 to look after all administrative matters, made use of this wing. Its officers at first were nobles of the highest rank, but later men of lower rank were recruited to perform the routine daily tasks. Documents were handed to the emperor at the end of a long stick fitted with a metal clamp that resembled a bird's bill. Before the emperor's arrival, the three table-like benches and the decorative chair lacquered in black (shown in the illustration) were placed in the main hall. The windows in the northwest wall are shaped like combs (Plate 47) and could be covered to ensure privacy.

In the western *hisashi* (Plate 39) a series of five rooms extending from south to north includes, first, the Oyudono-no-Ma, a waiting room for the emperor's bath attendants, and then a wash room, the Ochōsu-no-Ma (Plate 40). The Asagarei-no-Ma (Plate 43) is a pair of rooms where the emperor, at first, breakfasted and later came to take all his meals. It served also as a changing room, and so various ritualistic and ornamental objects were stored here for his use: combs and silver containers for hair oils, incense burners, and the like, as well as the chests that contained the Imperial crowns. (They are displayed to the public twice a year, in spring and autumn.) The fourth room in the west corridor, the Daiban-dokoro (Plate 44), contained a kitchen as well as a waiting room, and the last room, the Oni-no-Ma, was used by ladies-in-waiting.

The *moya*, the central chamber of the Seiryō-den, was not only part of the emperor's private living quarters but was also used on occasion in an official capacity for the conferring of court titles and the like. Here too the emperor and his court might come to enjoy the pleasures of *kangetsu* (moon-viewing) or to listen to music and poetry.

The *moya* contains both the Mi-Chō-Dai (the Imperial Curtained Throne), which the emperor used as a place of retirement, and the Dai-Shōji-no-Omashi (Plate 28) for the serving of food. Vivid descriptions of life in the Seiryō-den are given in many of the

⚹ DESCRIPTION

Japanese classics, such as *The Pillow Book, Kokinshū, The Tale of Genji,* and Lady Murasaki's diary.

In the eastern *hisashi* are several decorated screens, among them a silk screen by Tosa Mitsukiyo called the Konmeichi-no-Shōji (Plate 31) and the Arami-no-Shōji (Plates 33 and 34). Also by Tosa Mitsukiyo, this pair of sliding doors is decorated on the right with a winter scene, showing the bamboo baskets filled with stones that are used to dam the Uji River, while the left panel (enlarged in the illustration) shows two grotesquely deformed figures apparently preparing to ford a river.

Near the stairway are copies of the famous Nenjū-Gyōji-no-Shōji, which depict various annual festivities and recurring ceremonies in the life of the Imperial Palace. The originals were presented to Emperor Uda more than a millennium ago by a member of the Fujiwara clan, Mototsune, who became first Kwampaku of Japan, the chief dignitary at the Imperial Court.

Outside the west veranda is a sandy court planted with bush clover (Plate 38). The larger Eastern Garden, the Tō-tei, also has a white sandy floor, with two bamboo trees in wooden pots (Plates 35 and 36). In the background stand fruit trees, pines, and willows, as well as bush clover.

Beyond the Eastern Garden flows a small stream (Plate 37) that rises in Lake Biwa, which is so famous in Japanese poetry and painting. Long ago, at the Festival of the Dolls, it was the custom for the courtiers of the Palace to sit beside the stream and try to get a poem written before the wine cups that were floated down the river went past them. Then, after drinking wine by the water's edge, they adjourned to a party being held in one of the rooms of the Palace, where each courtier would make a present of his poem to one of the others.

PALACES OF KYOTO 炎

Leaving the Eastern Garden of the Seiryō-den and heading north across the Imperial Palace grounds, one encounters a series of palace buildings built almost in a straight line.

The first of these, the Ko-Gosho, or "Minor" Palace (Plate 57), has a central *moya* surrounded by the familiar wooden corridors of the *hisashi*; the style is a pleasant combination of the imposing and palatial *shinden-zukuri* with *shoin-zukuri,* domestic and religious architecture evolved during the Muromachi period (Plate 59).

The Ko-Gosho was associated with two ceremonies involving the prince Imperial (his assumption of manhood and his investiture) and was also the place customarily chosen by the emperor to meet his feudal lords. In the east courtyard the traditional ceremony took place of burning the first words that the emperor had written in the New Year. And it was here that Emperor Meiji convened the great assembly of lords that deprived the fifteenth Tokugawa shogun, Yoshinobu, of his power, which thus reverted into Imperial hands. That historic assembly marked the end of the Tokugawa military dictatorship in Japan and the beginning of the Meiji restoration.

The east corridor of the Ko-Gosho (Plate 58), with its outer railed veranda (Plate 61) is a typical example of the *shinden* style of Heian architecture, while the *ha-jitomi* doors are *shoin* in style. A painting from the northern *hisashi* is illustrated in Plate 60.

East of the Ko-Gosho lies the largest garden in the Imperial Palace, the O-Ike-Niwa, or Pond Garden (Plate 63). This was, and is, a favorite place for a quiet, meditative walk among the beautifully placed pines and maples. In the court just to the north of the Ko-Gosho, outside the corridor linking it to the Go-Gaku-monjo (Plate 64), lies the *kemari* (football) field of the Palace.

⚜ DESCRIPTION

The Go-Gakumonjo, originally constructed at the command of the famous, and infamous, Ieyasu, the first Tokugawa Shogun, closely resembles the Ko-Gosho in its combination of palatial and domestic styles (Plates 65 and 66). Like the latter, it faces east, with a roof sloping north and south; it is built of cypress wood; and it too has a hall divided into three rooms, with the Upper Room for the use of the emperor. The Chrysanthemum Room, the Yellow Rose Room, and the Wild Goose Room are all built in the *shoin* style, with coffered ceilings and low writing desks beneath windows looking onto the garden, while the veranda's railings and stairways suggest the *shinden* style.

As the name of the place suggests—*gakumon* means "learning" —it was used for Imperial lectures and poetry readings. Here, in 1860, Crown Prince Sachinomiya (later Emperor Meiji) chose to perform the ceremonies of his assumption of manhood. He was eight years old at the time.

North of the Go-Gakumonjo are the Omima-Goten and the Otsune-Goten, the two connected by a corridor. The Omima Palace, which faces south, was used for informal audiences as well as for certain special ceremonies, such as the anniversary of the death of the Buddha on February 15; the Bon Festival, a Buddhist holiday to commemorate the dead, in July; and the Tanabata Matsuri, or Star Festival, which celebrates the happy annual reunion of two stars, the Cowherd and the Weaver, who, though in love, were separated by the entire length of the Milky Way and came together only one night of the year. Apparently the festival dates back to the year 755, when the Empress-Regent Kōken commanded that it be celebrated in her presence and repeated every year thereafter on the seventh night of the seventh month.

43

PALACES OF KYOTO 业

Originally calculated by the lunar calendar, the date of the festival is now fixed on the night of July 7.

In times past, the emperor, from a room in the west corridor, used to watch the performance of Nō drama (the stage was torn down in 1945); and according to legend, Emperor Meiji learned to read and write in that same room. Some sliding doors from the Omima Palace are shown in Plate 72.

The Otsune-Goten (the "Ordinary Palace" or "Daily-Life Palace") contained the emperor's private apartments. The emperor had lived at first in the Jiju-den, then later in the Seiryō-den, but these Chinese-style buildings were considered uncomfortable, so at the command of Hideyoshi the first Otsune Palace was built in the *shoin* style as a place for the emperor to lead his private life. The facade is shown in Plate 68.

In the center of the building is the Imperial bedroom (an eighteen-mat room), with three audience-chambers south of it, called the Kenji-no-Ma (Plate 71). The Palace has fifteen rooms in all, with interior and exterior corridors on all sides and high railings. Details from some of the rooms are shown in Plates 69 and 70. South and east are wooden steps; below the southern steps lies a flower garden with white and red plum trees; while there is a larger and finer garden to the east, the Gonaitei, or Inner Court (Plate 74).

To the north and the east of the Otsune-Goten, lying amidst the shrubbery, is the Palace's earthquake shelter, the Jishin-den —a simple, even austere, but very beautiful little building roofed with cypress bark. Nearby is the Yatsu Bridge, two flat stones across the little stream that gives the Jishin-den its other name: The Cold-Water Spring Pavilion.

Continuing north from the Otsune-Goten, one comes next to the tiny Kōshun-Goten, the Palace of Coming Spring (Plate 73). Rebuilt during the middle of the nineteenth century at the command of Emperor Kōmei, he customarily used its two small rooms as his private library.

North again stands the Osuzumi-sho, "A-Place-to-be-Cool" (Plate 75), which, as its name indicates, was used by the emperor during the summer. The garden in front is called the Ryū-sen-no-Niwa. The Ue-no-oma (or Upper Room) is shown in Plate 76.

From here a roofed passage (Plate 77) leads to a teahouse known as the Chōsetsu, which was built in 1856 at Emperor Kōmei's command and to suit his taste. Set in the midst of a garden, far from the streets, in the innermost part of the Palace, it is so quiet that during the winter, snow can be heard falling—which is how the building got its name, for Chōsetsu means "Listening to Snow."

The Japanese word for a "teahouse" is *sukiya,* and that is the name given to the special style of architecture used for teahouses, which is always as simple as possible, in emulation of a Zen Buddhist monastery, where the monks, standing before an image of the Buddha, would all drink tea out of the same bowl—a custom that led, in the fifteenth century, to the development of the tea ceremony. Ceremonious tea-drinking in Japan, however, is far older, for Emperor Shōmu, who reigned in the eighth century, is known to have invited a hundred Buddhist monks to tea in the Imperial Palace. The tea-cult is regarded by its practitioners as a kind of discipline whose object is to induce the mental harmony prerequisite to enlightenment.

The tearoom itself, classically, has four and a half mats, the half-mat being placed in the center. The arrangement may be seen in the Chōsetsu tearoom illustrated in Plate 79. A stream passes under one corner of the house (Plate 81), and the Zen garden around it is a harmonious arrangement of rocks, moss, and white sand. A detail from the interior is shown in Plate 80.

To the west stands the Ohana-Goten, the Flower Palace, a *shoin*-style construction first built in 1809 for Crown Prince Ayahito (Emperor Ninkō) and used ever since by the crown princes. It is divided into four rooms, with a cypress-bark roof, eaves on all sides, and verandas to the north and the east. On one of the walls of the east room, called the Shikunshi-no-Ma, there are still vestiges of scribbling put there by Prince Sachinomiya, when he lived in the house and long before he became Emperor. The word *shikunshi,* after which the room is named, symbolizes the four "gentlemanly" plants: plum blossom, chrysanthemum, orchid, and bamboo.

Continuing west now, one reaches a pair of buildings inside the Seisho-mon—the Sannai-den and the Sōsha-dokoro. It was in the Sannai-den that ex-emperors, princes, and princesses exchanged their New Year's greetings; and the emperor himself came to watch the New Year's dance called the Senzu-Manzai when it was performed in the forecourt. For this he made use of the little structure, roofed with cypress bark, called the Okuruma-yose, which is where the higher-ranking people alighted who were allowed to enter the Palace in carriages (Plate 48).

In the east wing of the Sannai-den, the Kōtōnaishi had her office. She was a court lady of high rank who had charge of all the female personnel of the Imperial court, and it was she who issued permission to visitors who desired to enter the Otsune-Goten.

The Sōsha-dokoro was used mainly by attendants of the princes and peers who visited the Sannai-den, for which purpose there were several waiting rooms.

During the Second World War, the corridors of these buildings were dismantled, as a precaution against fire, but they are presently being restored to their original state.

At the northern end of the Palace, inside the Sakuhei-mon (Plate 85) is a group of buildings enclosed by a white wall. There used to be twelve in all, but after the court moved to Tokyo, many of the buildings fell into disrepair and only four are now still standing.

The first, approaching from the south, is the Kōgō-Goten, the private residence of the empress. In 1620, when the reigning Emperor was obliged to marry the daughter of the rich and powerful Tokugawa shogun, the Kōgō-Goten that she had built was at least as splendid as his own palace, but the present-day Kōgō-Goten is only about two-thirds the size of the Otsune-Goten.

The Imperial bedchamber is in the center of the building, with thirteen rooms around it. The Kurodo, in the north corridor, contains the Buddhist shrine of the household. All rooms have latticed ceilings, matted floors, sliding doors of painted cedar wood, and outer storm doors: the Kōgō Palace, in fact, though smaller than the Otsune, is very similar to it.

One of the distinctive features of the Kōgō-Goten is the use of attached writing-ledges, made in the old style, with alcoves beside them in which have been set shelves of the type illustrated in Plate 65. At night, the building can be closely shuttered on the outside by means of wooden panels running in grooves. The roof is the familiar cypress bark, there is a railed veranda on all four sides, and flights of steps on the east and the south.

PALACES OF KYOTO 火

To the north and to the west are the Wakamiya-Goten and the Himemiya-Goten, the former reserved for the use of the young princes, the latter for the young princesses. Both are designed in the *shoin* style, with verandas and interior eaves.

The northernmost building in the Palace is one of the most ancient. The Higyō-sha appeared in the first Heian construction, where it was reserved for the use of the *nyōgo*, the emperor's second wife, who ranked just after the empress, and in later years was often used as a residence by the empress herself and sometimes served as her hall of state.

The present structure is somewhat smaller than its Heian original, although it is built in the same *shinden* style, with a central *moya* surrounded by *hisashi* and railed verandas. The roof is thickly thatched and the eaves are supported by a double row of ribs that open out like a fan. One of the ceilings in the Higyō-sha is shown in Plate 83. At night the building is shut by latticed boards, the top halves of which can be raised for greater ventilation. In the north corridor is a room called the Denjōbito-no-Za, which in the past the peers sometimes used as a banquet hall; the south corridor gives onto a celebrated wisteria court (Plate 82).

Two more of the Imperial Palace structures must be mentioned, the Shunkō-den and the Shodaibu-no-Ma. The Shunkō-den (Plate 23) stands outside the Nikka gate that leads to the Shishin-den and for a long time was used as a sanctuary for the Imperial Regalia. It figured prominently in the enthronement ceremonies of the present Emperor. The building is of cypress wood, about forty feet by twenty-five, and is roofed with cedar bark.

The Shodaibu-no-Ma (Plate 49), which stands inside the Gishū gate of the west wall, was the building where those who were entitled to enter the Palace grounds riding in ox-drawn carriages waited until they were summoned to the Imperial presence. A painting from one of the waiting rooms is shown in Plate 50.

To the north is the Okuruma-yose (Plate 48), which was as far as the carriages customarily went, while to the south there now stands the Shin-kuruma-yose, built in 1915 for the enthronement ceremonies of Emperor Taishō. Its style does not blend too happily with the traditional architecture of the Imperial Palace.

Along the eastern wall stands a series of seven white-washed storerooms, where books, paintings, and documents dealing with the history of Kyoto and Japan are kept, as well as objects used in the enthronement ceremonies of the late Emperor Taishō and of the present Emperor and the appurtenances of such special Kyoto festivals as the Aoi-Matsuri. One of the storerooms, the Higashiyama-Bunko (East Mountain Storehouse), was moved to the Imperial Palace from the villa of the distinguished family of Konoe in Higashiyama. Among the treasures kept here are a scroll of Takashina Takakane, another depicting the Mongol invasion, manuscripts of Onono Tōfū and Kūkai, and bird paintings done by Maruyama Ōkyo. Although the other buildings of the Palace have burnt many times, the storerooms have luckily escaped, so their treasures are still intact.

Outside the actual precincts of the Imperial Palace stand two other royal palaces: the Sentō-Gosho, built as a private residence for ex-emperors, and the Ōmiya-Gosho, built for dowager-empresses and arch-dowager-empresses. Both palaces lie in a pine wood, southeast of the Imperial Palace, and both are encircled by the familiar *tsuijibei,* the tile-roofed earthwork wall.

Although very little of the Sentō Palace remains standing, its splendid gardens—many of them originally laid out by Kobori Enshū, one of Japan's master landscape-gardeners—give some hint of its magnificent past. The present gardens (Plates 90-96) are a re-evocation of the original gardens done during the reconstruction work ordered by Emperor Kōkaku in 1817.

The first construction arose after Emperor Go-Mizunoo, whose Empress was a Tokugawa, abdicated in favor of his daughter, who, at the age of seven, became, in 1629, one of the few female sovereigns to have ruled Japan. She reigned for thirteen years, then abdicated in her turn in favor of her younger brother, who became Emperor at the age of eleven and who died mysteriously ten years later. He was succeeded by another younger brother, who reigned for only seven years before abdicating in favor of a still younger sister, who was nine when she ascended the throne. It would seem to have been Tokugawa policy to keep Imperial power ostensibly in the hands of a minor so that it could be wielded in fact by the Tokugawas.

Meanwhile, the sire of this brood of princes, Go-Mizunoo, who had abdicated at the age of thirty-four, lived on for another half-century, and it was for him that the Sentō Palace was built. The site chosen was a familiar one to Imperial eyes, as a number of Fujiwara mansions had stood there. Construction began in 1626, while the Emperor was still on the throne, with the removal to the building site of the living quarters from Nijō Castle, which the Emperor had always used when he visited the castle. This served, apparently, as the core of the new Palace, which was not completed, however, until 1630, the year after the Emperor's abdication.

After the Great Fire of 1788, Sentō Palace was rebuilt more splendidly than ever and stood for almost seventy years, until it was again destroyed by fire in 1854. As there was no longer an ex-emperor living, the Palace was not rebuilt again, although its enclosing wall was reconstructed.

In 1915, on the accession of Emperor Taishō to the throne, the Daijō-Kyū was built in the northwest corner of the Sentō Palace grounds. It was here that the Daijō-Sai ceremony was performed on the occasion of the Emperor's enthronement, during the course of which he offered a cup of sacred rice to the Shinto gods, and the same ceremony was performed, in the same place, by the present Emperor on his enthronement in November, 1928.

There are several teahouses on the Palace grounds, among them the charming little Yūshin-tei (Plate 92), which was presented by the Konoe family; the classical five-roomed Seika-tei (Plates 94 and 95), with its very beautiful view over the South Pond and a forecourt where the outdoor tea ceremony was often performed; and the Kansui-tei, with another remarkable view over the water.

It is impossible to list all the various ponds, with their islands and bridges, the artificial hills with carefully placed trees, the man-made waterfalls and chasms, and the numerous Shinto shrines scattered over the grounds.

The Ōmiya-Gosho was first built in 1628 for the Tokugawa Empress Tōfukumon-in, wife of Emperor Go-Mizunoo, within a separate enclosure upon the grounds of the Sentō Palace. Three times it was burnt down and rebuilt; then it burnt again in the Great Fire of 1854, but unlike the Sentō Palace was rebuilt again, in

PALACES OF KYOTO 光

1867, in its original form for the Dowager Empress Hideteru, widow of Emperor Kōmei (Plates 88 and 89).

After its enlargement and refurbishing by Emperor Taishō, it has been used by members of the Imperial Family when they came to Kyoto, and it has also been offered to official guests of the nation, among them the Emperor of Abyssinia in 1956. At the present time, a group of national guests stays there every spring and autumn.

In 1747, the ex-emperor, Sakuramachi, asked his chief councillor to name the ten aspects of the grounds that he considered the most beautiful. This was the councillor's reply: "Cherry blossoms at Seika-tei, yellow roses around the old pond, rice shoots on the Hill of Longevity, fireflies over the fishing pavilion, the moon rising behind Yūzen-dai Hill, maple trees around the house by the waterfall, early winter rain falling softly on a thatched roof, snow on the Shishisai teahouse, a sunset reflected in the lake, candles flickering on the Shinto altars."

A SHORT COMPARATIVE CHRONOLOGY

EVENTS AT KYOTO	EVENTS IN THE WEST
794 Emperor Kanmu moves capital from Nara to Heian-kyō (Kyoto).	**732** Moors defeated at Battle of Poitiers.
805 Mt. Hiei becomes headquarters for Tendai sect of Buddhism.	**800** Charlemagne crowned.
860 Yoshifusa Fujiwara establishes dominion of Fujiwara over Imperial and temporal power. To last 300 years.	
941 Fujiwara Tadahira given total civil power.	**962** Foundation of Holy Roman Empire.
early 11th century *Tale of Genji* written by Murasaki Shikibu.	**1066** Norman invasion of England.
1155 Beginning of struggle for power between Taira and Minamoto clans.	
1167 Taira-no-Kiyomori conquers Kyoto and assumes total power as shogun.	
1185 Battle of Dan-no-Ura. Minamoto forces vanquish Taira. Minamoto Yoritomo establishes military government (shogunate) at Kamakura.	
1221 Retired Emperor Go-Toba defeated in uprising against shogunate.	**1215** Magna Carta. **1223** Genghis Khan conquers Asia.
1331 The Kyoto Imperial Palace moved to a noble's private residence—its present site.	**1271** Marco Polo starts his journey to Cathay. **1309–1417** Two popes and papal courts: Avignon and Rome.
1333 Emperor Go-Daigo defeats shogunate and briefly restores direct Imperial rule.	**1336** Outbreak of Hundred Years' War.
1335 Ashikaga Takauji declares himself shogun and moves shogunate to Kyoto.	**late 14th century** Conquests of Tamerlane. **ca. 1340–1400** Lifetime of Chaucer.

EVENTS AT KYOTO	EVENTS IN THE WEST
1336–92 Northern and Southern Imperial courts. **1368** Ashikaga Yoshimitsu becomes shogun. Golden age of art and literature. Zen Buddhism endorsed by shogunate. **1397** Golden Pavilion erected by Yoshimitsu. **15th century** Power of shogunate declines. **1469–87** Ōnin Rebellion. Kyoto devastated. Period of civil war begins. **1543** First Europeans arrive in Japan. **1549** St. Francis Xavier introduces Catholicism. **1567** Oda Nobunaga starts unification of country and captures Kyoto. **1587** Toyotomi Hideyoshi completes unification of country after Nobunaga's death. Art and culture flourish in Kyoto. **1600** Battle of Sekigahara. Tokugawa Ieyasu defeats Toyotomi forces and becomes shogun in 1603. **1610** Shogunate moved to Edo (Tokyo), but Kyoto remains Imperial capital until Meiji Restoration of 1868. **1639** End of "Christian century" in Japan; Japan closed. **1853** Arrival of American fleet under Commodore Perry. **1868** Shogun abdicates and Imperial rule restored. Capital moved to Edo, the name of which is changed to Tokyo.	**1453** Fall of Constantinople to the Turks. **1456** Gutenberg develops printing press with movable type. **1479** Spain united under Ferdinand and Isabella. **1492** Columbus discovers West Indies. **1517** Martin Luther launches Reformation. **1519–22** Magellan sails around the world. **1494–1566** Ottoman Empire flourishes under Suleiman. **1558** Accession of Elizabeth I to English throne. **1564** Birth of Shakespeare. **1618** Outbreak of Thirty Years' War. **1642** English Civil War. **late 17th century** Absolute monarchy of Louis XIV. **1683** Turks defeated at Vienna. **1685** Birth of Johann Sebastian Bach. **1775** Outbreak of American War of Independence. **1789** French Revolution **1793–1815** Napoleonic Wars. **1837** Accession of Queen Victoria **1859** Darwin's *Origin of Species* published. **1866** First successful transatlantic telegraph cable laid.

ANNUAL EVENTS CELEBRATED AT THE KYOTO IMPERIAL COURT

Tradition assigned certain events and celebrations to specific days of the yearly schedule of the ancient Imperial Court of Japan. The events of the year were recorded on a screen called the Nenjūgyoji-no-shōji, located under the eastern eaves of the Seiryō-den. This screen was first made in the reign of the Emperor Kōkō (884–887 A.D.) and has been remade after each of the many conflagrations. Some of the chief events celebrated:

Shihōhai ("Service of the Four Directions")—New Year's Day
The emperor, clad in a ceremonial court dress of black and yellow, stood in the east court of the Seiryō-den, worshiped the heaven, stars and Imperial ancestors, and prayed for peace and prosperity.

The origin of Shihōhai is not certain. It is ascribed to the reigns of the legendary Emperors Sujin (*ca.* 97–29 B.C.), Suinin (*ca.* 29–71 A.D.), and also to the Heian period Emperor Uda (887–897 A.D.).

Kochōhai (New Year's Service)—New Year's Day
It was customary for the emperor to receive greetings and congratulations from court officials at the Daigoku-den on New Year's Day. When this hall was destroyed by fire, the site of this ceremony was changed to the east court of the Seiryō-den during the reign of the Emperor Uda (887–897 A.D.).

Sechi-e ("Meeting of the Seasons" Banquet)—New Year's Day.
The New Year's Sechi-e is attributed to the Emperor Junna (823–833 A.D.) and was held at the Shishin-den. It was later discontinued.

Ao-uma-no-Sechi-e ("White Horse Banquet")—January 7
A Chinese tradition says that a white horse seen on the seventh day after the New Year means a propitious year to come. The Emperor Saga (809–823 A.D.) established a custom of viewing twenty white horses led through the courtyard of the Shishin-den, after which he gave a banquet for court officials.

Gokisho-Sagichō (Burning the Emperor's First Writings)—January 15
This ceremony took place in the east court of the Ko-Gosho, where three bamboo poles were set up, from which folding fans with the emperor's New Year's writings were hung. The fans were then burned with sacred fire.

Tōka-no-Sechi-e ("Dance and Song Banquet")—January 18
This event was held in the court of the Shishin-den where the emperor witnessed a musical and dance display by forty-six girls. Said to have been initiated in the reign of the Emperor Jitō (686–697 A.D.), the number of dancers diminished to two in the Edo period. The emperor gave a banquet after the entertainment.

Kasuga Matsuri (*matsuri* means "festival")—March 13
The emperor used to dispatch an Imperial messenger to the Kasuga Shrine in Nara on March 13 to attend the Kasuga Matsuri. This Festival is still held today and has become increasingly popular. Actors in the Festival are dispatched from Kyoto even today.

The Kasuga Shrine was patronized by the Fujiwara family, and it is said that the Festival was initiated in 850 A.D. On this day, four treasures of the Shrine, a halberd, sword, mirror and bow, are exhibited.

Aoi Matsuri (Hollyhock Festival)—May 15
The grand Aoi Matsuri is held on May 15 every year with a procession of five hundred persons clad in ancient court costume winding its way from the Kyoto Gosho to the Shimogamo and Kamigamo shrines. It is a colorful pageant reminiscent of the splendor of the Heian period (see pictures page 156).

Iwashimizu Matsuri—September 15
The Iwashimizu Matsuri is a festival held at the Iwashimizu Hachiman Shrine in the suburbs of Kyoto on September 15. A procession of men and women clad in ancient court attire winds its way from Kyoto to the Shrine in this Festival. It was first held on the fifteenth day of the eighth month (lunar calendar) in 863.

Yoori-no-Gi ("Severing of Seasons" Ceremony)—June 30 and December 31
This is a ceremony held twice a year, on June 30 and December 31, aimed at driving out the evils of each half-year period. The ceremony, according to legend, dates back to the goddess Izanami.

Niiname-sai ("Tasting of First Fruits" Ceremony)—November 23
On this day, the Emperor offers the newly harvested rice to Amaterasu Omikami and other ancient gods at the Shinka-den and also partakes of the new rice that day.

Tsuina ("Exorcism")—Last day of December
A ceremony to drive out all evils of the past year was held by the emperor in the Imperial Palace. One of the events is the Tsuina, a ceremony to exorcise evil spirits, based on Chinese tradition.

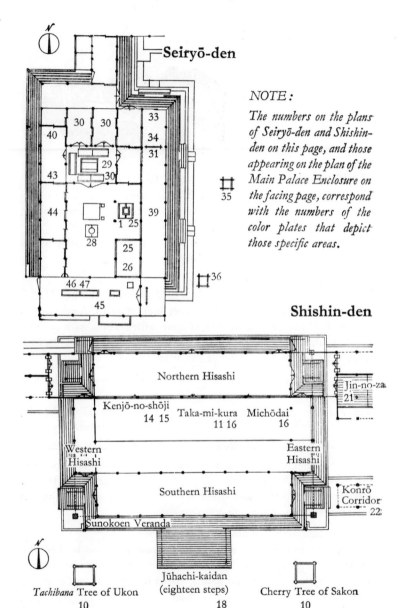

Seiryō-den

NOTE:

The numbers on the plans of Seiryō-den and Shishin-den on this page, and those appearing on the plan of the Main Palace Enclosure on the facing page, correspond with the numbers of the color plates that depict those specific areas.

30 30 33

40 34

31

29

43 30

35

44 39

1 25

28

25

26

46 47 36

45

Shishin-den

Northern Hisashi

Jin-no-za
21

Kenjō-no-shōji
14 15 Taka-mi-kura Michōdai
11 16 16

Western
Hisashi

Eastern
Hisashi

Southern Hisashi

Konrō
Corridor
22

Sunokoen Veranda

Tachibana Tree of Ukon
10

Jūhachi-kaidan
(eighteen steps)
18

Cherry Tree of Sakon
10

Plan of the Main Palace Enclosure

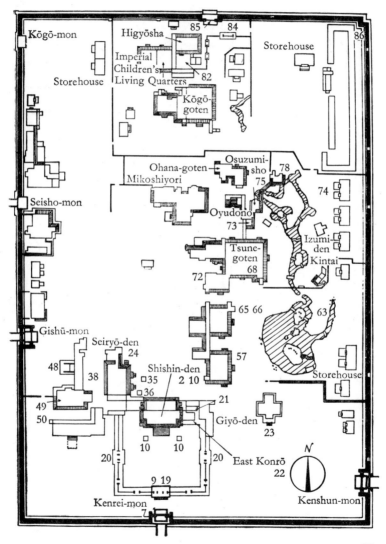

Kōgō-mon

Higyōsha 85 84

Storehouse 86

Storehouse

Imperial Children's Living Quarters 82

Kōgō-goten

Osuzumi-sho 78

Ohana-goten 75

Mikoshiyori 74

Seisho-mon

Oyudono 73

Izumi-den

Kintai

Tsune-goten 68

72

65 66

63

Gishū-mon

Seiryō-den 24

Storehouse

48

38

Shishin-den 35 2 10

36

57

49

50

21

Giyō-den

10 10

23

20 20

East Konrō 22

9 19

N

Kenrei-mon

Kenshun-mon

7

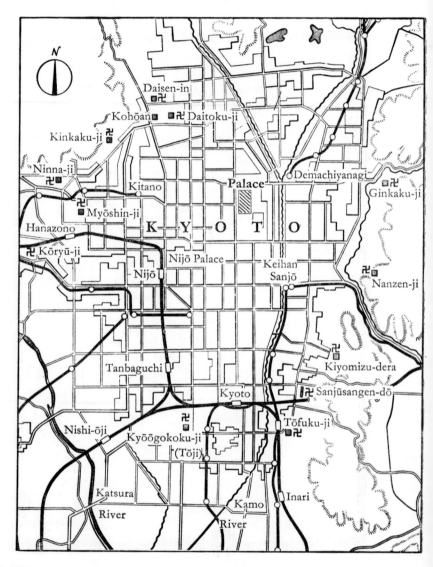

N

Daisen-in

Kohōan 卍 Daitoku-ji

Kinkaku-ji 卍

Ninna-ji 卍

Kitano

Palace

Demachiyanagi

Ginkaku-ji 卍

Myōshin-ji 卍

K Y O T O

Hanazono

Kōryū-ji 卍

Nijō Palace

Nijō

Keihan
Sanjō

Nanzen-ji 卍

Tanbaguchi

Kiyomizu-dera

Kyoto

Sanjūsangen-dō 卍

Nishi-ōji

Kyōōgokoku-ji
(Tōji) 卍

Tōfuku-ji 卍

Katsura
River

Kamo
River

Inari

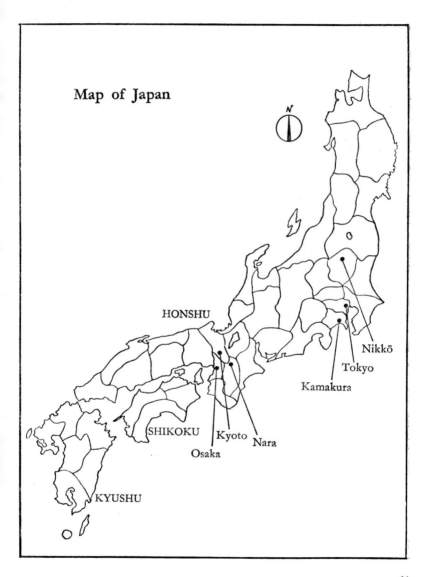

Map of Japan

N

HONSHU

Nikkō

Tokyo

Kamakura

SHIKOKU   Kyoto

Nara

Osaka

KYUSHU

5. *Earthwork walls* with tiled ▶
roofs that enclose the Imperial
Palace grounds are called
tsuijibei: earth-colored, they
have five white horizontal lines
and enclose a total area of
about twenty-seven acres.

6. *Imperial Palace at Kyoto* (*see over-leaf*), with its own *tsuijibei*, has a main palace area of over twenty-seven acres. The constructions are all one-storied, most of them with sloping roofs of cypress bark.

7. *Kenrei-mon* (*above*) is the southern, and principal, gate to the Palace. Its doors are opened only for the emperor.

8. *Hana-hazama* is the Japanese name for the decorative panels found in the upper halves of the gates. Below is the carved *hana-hazama* of the Kenrei-mon.

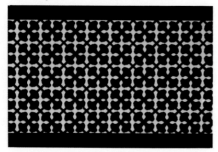

9. *The main gate* of the Shishin-den ▶ is called the Jōmei-mon and opens onto the southern front of the courtyard. Its red-lacquered columns and tiled roof are both characteristic features of architecture of the Heian period in the eighth and ninth centuries.

10. *Facade of Shishin-den* (*see preceding page*), the heart of the Palace. The style is also traditionally Heian, with its cypress bark roof and wide eaves.

11. *The Imperial Throne* (*above*) in the main hall of the Shishin-den is called the Taka-mi-kura. Phoenix-like birds decorate its canopy.

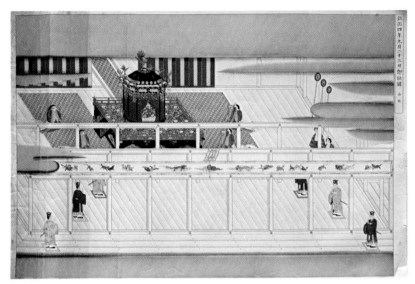

12. *Painted panel* of the enthronement of Emperor Kōmei, which took place in the Shishin-den on September 23, 1847. Men wore *sokutai* and women wore *jūni-hitoe*.

13. *The Imperial Throne* in the Shishin-den (the Goishi) is made of red sandalwood, lacquered and inlaid with mother-of-pearl. The cushion is covered in heavy silk brocade.

14. *Chang-hua,* a famous scholar of the Han dynasty, is one of the thirty-two sages of China painted on eight sliding screens behind the Imperial Throne in the Shishin-den.

16. *Main hall of the Shishin-den*▶
called the *moya (see overleaf)*,
showing the emperor's throne in
the foreground and behind it that
of the empress. These were constructed for the enthronement
ceremonies of Emperor Taishō in
1915, after original models.

15. *Four Chinese sages,* from the
same screens. They were first
painted by Kose Kanaoka at the
command of Emperor Uda in 892
—and have been repainted as often
as they have been destroyed.

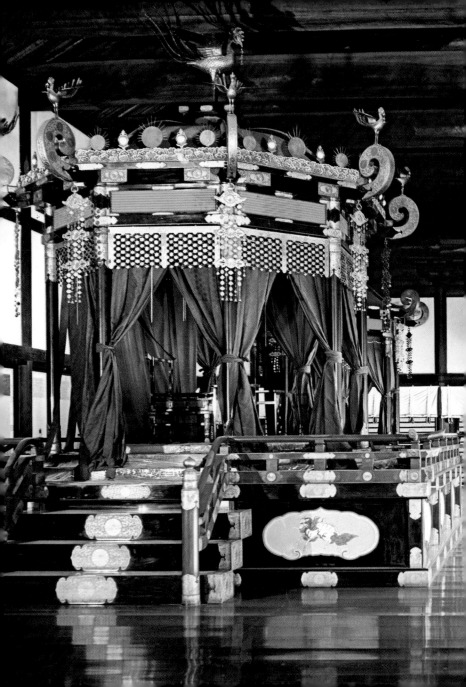

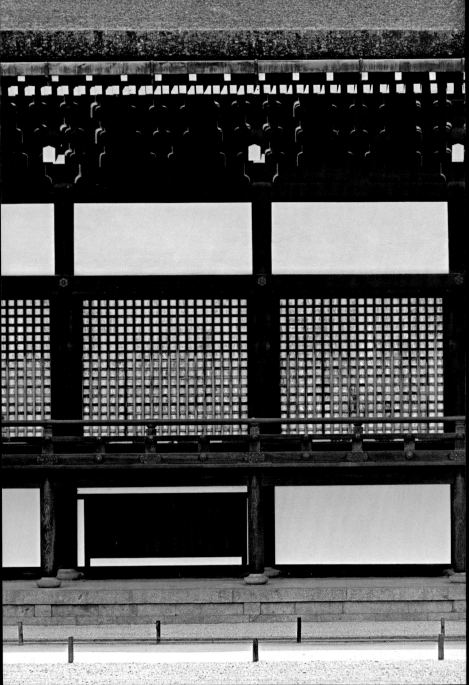

17. *North stairway* of the Shishin-den which leads to the north corridor behind the emperor's throne. The stairway has nine steps, with a railing on one side, for the number nine was considered in Chinese philosophy to be the final number and the holiest.

19. *Jōmei-mon,* the main entrance to the Shishin-den, with part of the outer corridor around the Shishin-den courtyard. The roof is tiled over white walls, with supporting columns lacquered vermilion; the effect, against the white sand of the courtyard, is striking.

20. *Sunflower Gate* as seen from Moonflower Gate across the courtyard of the Shishin-den. These are the east and west gates, respectively, of the Shishin-den Palace, and their columns are lacquered vermilion.

◀18. *"The eighteen steps"* (Jūhachi-kaidan) that lead from the southern, sandy courtyard of the Shishin-den to the main hall are made of cypress, with an easy rise to facilitate the bearing of the imperial carriage.

21. *Jin-no-Za,* across the court from the Konrō Corridor (*see* Plate 22, opposite), was used in times past by Imperial ministers, who made many of their most important decisions here, and also by the Imperial Guard whenever the emperor appeared. The screen is by Sumiyoshi Hirotaka.

23. *The Imperial Regalia,* consisting ▶ of the three sacred treasures, the sword, the jewel, and the mirror, are brought from the Palace in Tokyo to Kyoto when an enthronement ceremony is being performed and are kept in this sanctuary, called the Shunkō-den.

22. *The Konrō Corridor* connects the Shishin-den with the Giyō-den and is used only for special ceremonies connected with the emperor, such as the selecting of a site for the sacred rice field to be dedicated to the Imperial Ancestral Shrine.

24. *Seiryō-den* ("the pure cool hall") was used, until the middle of the Heian period, as the emperor's private residence, and since it was not built for ceremonial

purposes, it is more compact and orderly than the
Shishin-den. It furnished the locale for much classical
Japanese literature.

25. *The East Corridor* of the Seiryō-den: the marble rectangle is the Ishi-bai-dan, where the emperor came daily to pay homage to the Grand Shrine of Ise, and beyond it the two thick mats with embroidered cushion where he customarily sat during the day (Hi-no-omashi).

85

26. *The circular red board* in the Ishibai-dan (*see* Plate 25) was called the Chiri-tsubo, but was also known by the name of Jiro. It could be removed and the area underneath was used in the winter as a hearth; at other times it served as a kind of dust-collector.

27. *Open veranda* outside the east▶ corridor of the Seiryō-den where, in times past, Imperial ministers stood in audience before the emperor, who sat in the Hi-no-omashi (*see* Plate 25); in their long formal court robes, they made a colorful spectacle.

28. *Daishōji-no-omashi,* also in the Seiryō-den: here, on these two low benches with matted tops and on the red-lacquered table, food was served for the New Year's feast as well as for certain other formal occasions.

29. *An Imperial bedroom* north of the central hall of the Seiryō-den: the bed consists of three thick *tatami* mats with one lying on top of the other two. This room, unlike many of the others, has a wall of its own.

30. *In the north corridor* of the Seiryō-den are these two plain but handsome un-matted rooms. The one on the left was used by the emperor himself; that on the right by his consorts.

31. *This silk screen* in the east corridor was painted by Tosa Mitsukiyo and depicts a famous Chinese pond, the Konmeichi, from which the screen takes its name; the reverse side shows a hawk-hunting scene at Sagano.

32. *A room in the Seiryō-den* built in▶ the more palatial style called *shinden* and showing two types of doors used in the Imperial Palace: the *orijitomi*, a hinged door that folds upward, and the ordinary paneled door, called the *tsumado*.

33–34. *A pair of sliding doors* in
the northern end of the east corridor of the Seiryō-den, done in
India ink by Tosa Mitsukiyo.
Sei Shōnagon, who wrote "The
Pillow Book" in the tenth century, describes the distaste these
pictures evoked in the court
ladies of her time. At left is a
detail of the screen.

35–36. *Bamboo plants* in the east courtyard of the Seiryō-den (*see* Plate 24). Plate 35 shows the variety called *kure-take* (*Han* bamboo), which has narrower leaves than the *kawa-take* (*wu* bamboo), shown in Plate 36. The emperor used to come to this courtyard to watch the New Year's dances and the Aoi festival, and sometimes a moon-viewing banquet was held here.

漢竹

37. *A small stream* from Lake Biwa flows through the eastern part of the Seiryō-den grounds. Here it is shown channeled, in the grounds of the Koki-den, with the ground level lowered to form a tiny waterfall.

38. *Bush clover courtyard,* beyond the west veranda of the Seiryō-den, with an enclosed corridor in the background. In the spring, the clover puts out fresh young leaves and in the autumn magnificent flowers—both of which look well against the white-sand court.

39. *West corridor* of the Seiryō-den, showing the open veranda and five rooms that were used by the emperor, the Imperial consorts, and their ladies-in-waiting.

40. *A room in the Seiryō-den* where the emperor, after he had dressed in the morning, came to wash his hands.

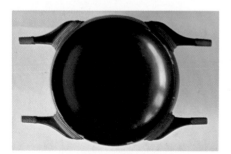

41. *The Tsunodarai (above)* takes its name from its pair of horn-shaped handles; *tsuno* is the Japanese word for "horn."

◀42. *Decorative silver container* for oil, left, used by the emperor when he combed his hair.

43. *A pair of rooms* in the Seiryō-den, used as a dressing-room by the emperor, and also on occasion as a breakfast room.

44. *Daiban-dokoro,* in the west corridor of the Seiryō-den, served for the preparation of the emperor's meals and also as a waiting-room for the ladies of the court.

46–47. *Comb-shaped windows* in the ▶ Seiryō-den.

45. *A meeting-room* in the Seiryō-den, where much ministerial business was conducted in the past. The three wooden tables are lacquered in vermilion. The lower floor was used by lesser officials.

49. *Customary waiting-rooms* for ▶ peers were in the Shodaibu-no-ma, where each noble had to use the room to which his rank entitled him. These had names like Tiger Room, Crane Room and Cherry Tree Room, in that order of importance.

48. *Noblemen* who were permitted to enter the Palace, through the Gishu-mon, in ox-drawn carriages halted here, at the Okuruma-yose, where corridors allowed them to pass to other buildings in the Palace compound.

50. *Tiger room* was used by nobles who were councillors of state. The painting is by Gantai.

106

51. *"Everlasting Summer"* is the name of this
screen, painted by an artist of the Kanō school
during the Edo period and illustrating a scene
from Lady Murasaki's classic novel, *The Tale
of Genji*, written in the eleventh century about
court life in Kyoto and the loves of Prince
Genji.

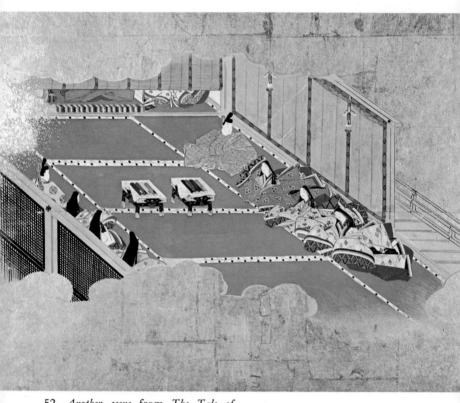

52. *Another scene* from *The Tale of Genji*, this screen depicts nobles of the court enjoying a favorite pastime, a private showing of well-known painted scrolls.

53. *"The Flower Party,"* done by the famous Tanyū of the Kanō school of painting, shows a cherry-blossom viewing-party in the spring, just after the trees have burst into bloom.

55. *Gosechi dancer,* one of five daughters of noble families, who, after an enthronement ceremony, dance to the accompaniment of court music played by the Imperial musicians.

◄54. *Jūni-hitoe* is the colorful ceremonial robe worn by the ladies of the court: it is made up of twelve kimonos, all with special names. The costume re-evokes ancient Japan, unlike the clothes of the Nara period, adapted from the Chinese.

56. *Sokutai,* illustrated here, is the ceremonial robe worn by noblemen at court; the color of the robe was determined by the rank of the wearer. He also carried a crown and a sword.

57. *Ko-Gosho* (The "Minor" Palace) was first built for the son of a Kamakura shogun; in 1251, its style was copied for Imperial use. In 1954, as a result of a fireworks display on the Kamo River, the Palace burnt down; by

November, 1958, its restoration to its original form was completed. Its cypress bark roof, railed corridors, and door-shaped latticed panels are all characteristic features of the *shinden* style.

58. *East Corridor* of Ko-Gosho: it was in this building that the ceremonies of the assumption of manhood by a prince and the investiture of the Prince Imperial were performed. And here, in the east corridor, Emperor Meiji acceded to the throne on January 9, 1867.

59. *The Upper Room* of the main hall of Ko-Gosho. Like many of the palaces, the main hall is divided into upper, middle, and lower rooms; the emperor's throne was placed in the upper room. The rooms are divided by sliding doors, and all have coffered ceilings.

60. *Hawk-hunting Scene,* taken from ▶ one of the sliding doors in the north corridor of Ko-Gosho. The artist is Reizei Tameyasu.

61. *East corridor* of Ko-Gosho, with its outer railed veranda, is typical of the *shinden* style used in Imperial buildings. It was in the Ko-Gosho that the emperor customarily gave audience to the daimyo.

62. *Ha-jitomi doors* in the east veranda of Ko-Gosho are survivals of the *shoin* style. These are latticed doors, of which the upper half may be raised for increased ventilation.

63. *The Pond Garden* (*see preceding page*) stands outside the eastern side of Ko-Gosho. It was designed in 1620 by the famous landscape gardener, Kobori Enshū, who was given a free hand in the arrangements. The banks of the pond are made of pebbles and white sand.

64. *Roofed corridor* (*below*) joins Ko-Gosho with the Palace just north of it, the Go-Gakumonjo, and was used by the emperor in order to proceed to the Shishin-den whenever a special ceremony was performed. *Kemari*, a type of football, was played in the court outside.

65. *Chidori-dana* shelves in the Chrysanthemum Room of Go-Gakumon-jo, a particular type of Japanese shelf-construction in which the shelves overlap in the center. On occasion the sacred sword and jewel of the Imperial Regalia have been kept here.

66. *Upper Room* of Go-Gaku-monjo, with matted floor and staggered shelves. In the center are two mats with a magnificently embroidered cushion for the use of the emperor. Here he performed the New Year's writing ceremony, following which the words were burnt. Paintings are by Kanō Eigaku.

68. *Otsune-Goten* was the name given to the ▶
Palace built in the sixteenth century in the
domestic *shoin* style as a place where the
emperor might spend his private life in more
comfort than was possible in the more ceremonious, Chinese-style palaces. There are
fifteen rooms in all.

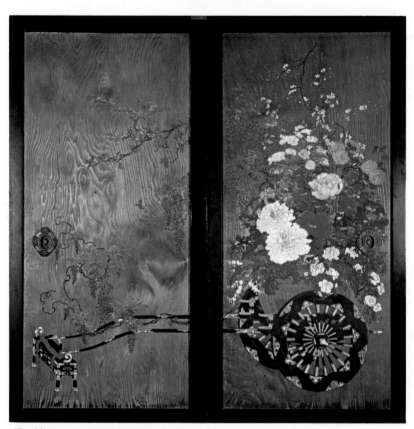

67. *Sliding doors* of cedar wood
from the east veranda. The flower
cart was painted by Yoshida
Kōkin.

69–70. *Sliding cedarwood* doors of Otsune-
Goten are famous for their painted
panels. Above is a scene known as
"Homecoming" by Mori Kansai, from
the Chinese poem *Kueichilai*, while to the
right is a painting by Isono Kadō done
in 1855 of a hawk clinging to a pine tree.

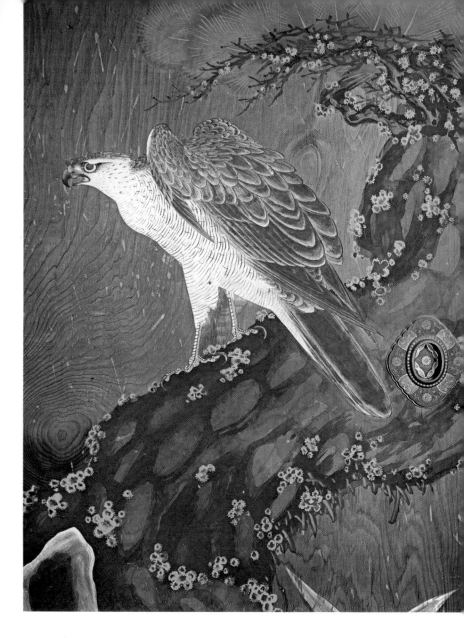

71. *Kenji-no-Ma,* the three-roomed audience chamber of the Tsune-Goten, which takes its name from the fact that two of the three treasures that constitute the Imperial Regalia, the sword and the jewel (*kenji*), are housed here. All three rooms are eighteen mats. The panels show scenes from Chinese history.

72. *New Year's Ceremony* at Daigoku-den, painted on sliding doors by Hirotaka of the Sumiyoshi school of painting. The doors are to be found in one of the north rooms of the Omima-Goten.

73. *Palace of Coming Spring*: shown here is the larger of its two rooms, one of ten mats (the other is only four mats), with painted panels of animals against the wall. There are verandas on all four sides.

74. *Inner Garden* is the name given ▶ to the lovely garden on the east side of the Otsune-Goten. If you cross the bridge and follow the path a little further, you will reach a teahouse standing on an artificial hill.

75. *"A-Place-to-be-Cool"* (Osuzu-mi-sho) faces east, and its four rooms were so well ventilated that they were airy and cool even in the heat of a Kyoto summer. There are verandas on both the south and east, which look over the Inner Garden.

76. *One of the rooms* of the Osu-zumi-sho. The paintings on the wall are the work of Tamura Kyoshū. The east veranda looks onto an arbor with a little pond —a most inviting place to spend a summer evening.

78. *Chōsetsu Teahouse* is a shingle-▶
roofed building of rustic style with
but two small rooms—one of four-
and-a-half mats and one of three.
The style, called Sukiya, is chosen
deliberately to encourage the harmony between man and nature
that the ceremonious serving of
tea is supposed to induce.

77. *Open corridor* leading from
Osuzumi-sho to the Chōsetsu
teahouse. A stream passes underneath. The day before Emperor
Meiji left Kyoto for Tokyo he
wrote a poem expressing his
sadness that he would have only
one more night to hear the sound
of the stream murmuring its way
under the corridor.

79. *A room in Chōsetsu,* with four scenes of one summer day, from morning to night, painted on the doors and screens. The cormorants fishing at left represent evening. The building is as simply furnished as possible. The two framed characters that say Chōsetsu are the work of Konoe Tadahiro.

81. *North garden of Chōsetsu (below)* is called Katatsumuri-no-niwa (The Snail Garden) because its shape, with the moss island surrounded by white sand, is thought to resemble a snail.

80. *Above,* a maple-leaf-shaped cloisonné door pull in Chōsetsu.

82. *Higyō-sha, the Wisteria Garden.* Many classical Japanese poems allude to the beauty of the wisteria blossoms here, which have been famous for over a thousand years, and the building itself is mentioned often in Heian literature.

142

83. *Beamed ceiling of Higyō-sha,* done in the *shinden* style. The thickly thatched roof, railed verandas, *shitomi-do* windows, and columns of cypress wood are also characteristic of this style.

143

84. *Genki-mon* (*above*), just inside the northern gate (the Sakuhei-mon, *see below*) of the Imperial Palace, was reserved for the use of the empress, since it led to her private residence, the Kōgō-Goten.

85. *Sakuhei-mon* is the principal gate of the north wall, opposite the Kenrei-mon of the south wall. Four columns support the cypress bark roof. The gate was opened for the installation ceremonies of 1868.

86. *Ki-mon* (*above*), at the northeast corner of the *tsuijibei,* is the gate through which evil spirits might pass into the Palace, for northeast has always been considered an unlucky direction in Japan.

87. *A monkey,* sacred to the deity of Hiei, guards the Ki-mon. He stands on a fork-shaped frame, wears the headdress of a court noble, and brandishes a staff with fluttering papers to ward off demons. The wire net is to keep him from running away.

88. *Ōmiya-Gosho* fell into complete disrepair after 1872, when the Dowager Empress joined the rest of the Imperial Family in Tokyo; in 1854 all of its chief buildings had been demolished save for the Tsune-Goten. After Emperor Taishō acceded to the throne in 1915, however, he added eight rooms to the Tsune-Goten for the use of the Imperial Family.

146

89. *Ōmiya-Gosho garden (below)*, with white and red plum trees. The grounds where the Ōmiya Palace and the remains of the Sentō Palace stand occupy some two hundred and fifty acres and boast many famous rock gardens, orchards, ponds with islands and bridges, and teahouses.

90. *Garden in Sentō Palace* grounds (*see overleaf*), one of many. Construction of the Palace began in 1626, on a Fujiwara site, and was completed in 1630, the year following the abdica-tion of Emperor Go-Mizunoo, for ▶ whom it was built. The gardens were finished in 1634 under the direction of Kobori Enshū, probably Japan's most famous landscaper.

91. Striped bamboo plants.

93. *Yatsu Hashi,* a bridge over the South Pond of Sentō Palace, is shaped like the Japanese phonetic sign in *hiragana,* " く ".▶

92. *Yūshin-tei, below,* a teahouse presented by the Konoe family after the Shishisai teahouse burnt down. The Sentō Palace has often been destroyed by fire (three times in one fifteen-year period).

94. Seika-tei teahouse as seen across ▶
the South Pond of Sentō Palace.

95. *The name Seika-tei* was taken from one of Rihaku's poems about a man who drinks too much wine in the moonlight and sobers up in the morning when he sees a beautiful flower, for "Seika-tei" means "Hangover-flower Teahouse." Below is one of the five tearooms in the building.

96. *Pebbled pond* in Sentō Palace ▶ (*see overleaf*). The egg-shaped pebbles were collected and presented by Lord Ōkubo, of the Odawara family, who paid for each one *shō* of rice—a measure equal to about a quart and a half.

AOI FESTIVAL

97. *Saiō on her way* to the Kamo shrines for the Aoi Festival; this began thirteen hundred years ago when Emperor Kinmei went to propitiate the deities of the shrines whose anger was thought to be causing the terrible storms that were ravaging the country.

98. *The festival* duplicates ancient Imperial processions. About five hundred people, all wearing hollyhock (*aoi*) and dressed in costumes of the Heian period, parade from the Palace to the shrines, where ceremonies are performed.

99. *Gissha (the ox-drawn carriage)*, decorated with artificial flowers, proceeds toward the shrines. The festival lapsed during the turbulent Muromachi period but was revived in 1694, and in 1884, the 17th year of the reign of Emperor Meiji, May 15th was fixed upon as its permanent date.

THIS BEAUTIFUL WORLD